FOREIGN TO FAMILIAR

A GUIDE TO UNDERSTANDING HOT- AND COLD-CLIMATE CULTURES

BY

SARAH A. LANIER

Published by:

McDougal Publishing
P.O. Box 3595
Hagerstown, MD   21742-3595
USA

www.mcdougalpublishing.com
978-1-58158-022-8
Previously 1-58158-022-3

Revised Edition 2010
Reprint 2014

Printed in the United States of America
For Worldwide Distribution
For additional copies of *Foreign to Familiar,* please
contact McDougal Publishing:
1-800-9MCDOUGAL
1-800-962-3684

ACKNOWLEDGMENTS

I want to acknowledge the extraordinary efforts of Ricardo Rodriguez, who took scores of hours to explain to me how Latin leaders think, and who believed the effort was worth his time.

I want to thank Darlene Cunningham and Floyd McClung, my mentors in leadership, and my inspiration to love the nations.

I also want to acknowledge the countless friends who pestered me to get my lectures into book form ... until I did. You know who you are.

DEDICATION

To my parents, Chandler and Sallie Lanier, who brought me to live in the Middle East as a child, and showed me the joy of loving people of other cultures. They also showed me that as I commit my way to God, He will direct my path.

CONTENTS

Correspondence with the author may be directed to:

Sarah A. Lanier
P O Box 874
Clarkesville, GA 30523
USA

sarah_a_lanier@yahoo.com

For editions in the following languages, please contact the author at the above address.

Arabic
French
German
Korean
Norwegian
Russian
Spanish

PREFACE

The Delta flight was leaving on time. Three of us were strapped in, one next to the other, each finding it easy to make small talk. As the plane lifted off, so did our burdens of office work. We were off to Glorietta, New Mexico, for a week-long conference, and our minds were filled with thoughts of mountains and crisp air and a break from the Atlanta downtown routine.

"So, Sarah," my aisle-seat colleague said in that chatty manner of a tourist on vacation, "tell me what it was like growing up in Israel."

Of all conversation openers, this was my least favorite. I'd been hearing it ever since moving to the States to begin my university studies. But, being in the middle seat, I couldn't escape.

My desire was to respond, "No, you first. Tell me what it was like growing up in a ranch-style house in suburbia." What was there to say? And who cares anyway?

But I did answer … well, sort of. "It was great," was the extent of my glib answer.

"No, I mean it, really," she insisted. "What is the culture like over there?"

By the window sat Aida from Lebanon. She'd been in the States eight years and was much more of an expert on Middle Eastern culture than I was. But, at the moment, Aida seemed to be fascinated by the window. So I took up the challenge.

"Well, I grew up in a variety of cultures. The Jewish and Arab cultures are vastly different."

"How so?" she asked.

"In the Jewish culture, you say what you think. It's direct, and you know where you stand with people."

I glanced at her to see if she was still with me. She was, so I continued.

"The Arab culture, on the other hand, is much more indirect. It's all about friendliness and politeness. If offered a cup of coffee, I say 'No, thank you.'

"The host offers it again, and I decline again with

something like: 'No, no, don't bother yourself.' He might offer a third time, and I'd reply, "No, I really don't want any coffee. Believe me.'

"Then my host serves the coffee, and I drink it."

"You've got to be kidding!" she said, incredulously.

"No, really," I assured her. "You're supposed to refuse the first few times. It's the polite thing to do."

"Then, what if you really don't want the coffee?" she asked.

"Well, then there are idioms you can use to say that you wouldn't for any reason refuse their kind hospitality, and at some point in the future you'll gladly join them in coffee, but at the moment you really can't drink it."

Now Aida got into the conversation. "Incredible! I didn't know that!" she said, as our heads turned her way.

"Aida," I replied, "what do you mean you didn't know that? You're Lebanese, for heaven's sake."

"Yes," she said, "but I mean I didn't know this was not normal. I've been in the United States eight years

9

already, and did not realize it was done differently here. That explains so much.

"I've been lonely since moving here, and now I know why. When people in the office would ask me if I wanted to go to lunch, I would say 'no' to be polite, fully expecting them to ask me again. When they didn't and left without me, I thought they didn't really want me along and had asked only out of politeness. In my culture, it would have been too forward to say 'yes' the first time.

"For this reason, I've had few American friends. After all these years, now I know why."

I sat there stunned. Pondering the sadness of her story, I said to myself, "No one should have to suffer like that simply because they don't understand the culture of another."

For the Aidas around the world, I have written this book.

Sarah A. Lanier

INTRODUCTION

The world is getting smaller as more people are traveling, immigrating, fleeing war zones and working overseas. This movement is creating cross-cultural encounters at a mind-boggling rate. Modern media and the Internet contribute to the blurring of cultural borders, leading us to think there are few cultural differences. In relating to one another, however, the truth soon becomes apparent. Hostilities quickly flare as ethnic groups become polarized and cultural identities are defended.

People are going overseas now more than any other time in history. However, although getting there is easy, knowing how to connect in friendship with the people they meet or live among is quite another matter. Even when people come home glowing about the great response they had among the people of some other land, they rarely know the other side of the story: the confusion they may have left in their wake. Relatively few people who try to work with those of other cultures understand that the way they live out their values and customs is probably completely foreign to those they are relating to. They can expect the values and customs of others to be completely foreign to them as well.

No one book could ever serve as a resource for all the cultural practices of the peoples of the earth, and this one does not pretend to do so. I have found, however, that there are generalizations about groups of people that actually do help.

Cultural differences among us provide both the richest color to our lives and the harshest wounding. Simple communication creates conflict. Innocent comments produce withdrawal and gossip. Living and working with people of different cultures used to be a novelty, but no longer. Virtually everywhere we turn, we encounter people with very different values and customs, and we often find them to be offensive.

The average cross-cultural worker has few cross-cultural skills and, in some cases, does not even see the need to acquire them. The sad thing is that his or her good intentions can be read wrongly, damaging relationship with colleagues without knowing it.

I have put forth this little handbook of cultural observations in response to repeated requests to do so when I lecture on the subject. The book divides the world into two halves: hot-climate cultures and cold-climate cultures, making generalizations that prove to be helpful if taken as that: generalizations. I trust that it will be helpful to those who wish to cross the culture gap.

My Countrymen

With respect to my countrymen ... I have studied their character with attention. ... I had even ascribed this to its cause, to that warmth of their climate which unnerves and unmans both body and mind. While on this subject I will give you my idea of the characters of the several states. In the North they are: cool, sober, laborious, persevering, independent, jealous of their own liberties and just to those of others, interested, chicaning, superstitious and hypocritical in their religion. In the South they are: fiery, voluptuary, indolent, unsteady, independent, zealous for their own liberties, but trampling on those of others, generous, candid, without attachment or pretensions to any religion but that of the heart.

These characteristics grow weaker and weaker by gradation from North to South and South to North, insomuch that an observing traveller, without the aid of the quadrant, may always know his latitude by the character of the people among whom he finds himself.

Thomas Jefferson

(Written to the Marquis of Chastellux, 2 September, 1785)

CHAPTER ONE

HOT-
VERSUS
COLD-CLIMATE CULTURES

The observation that people of different cultures think, act and react differently is nothing new. Anyone who travels or knows someone from abroad has observed this phenomenon. In my own country, the observation was made as early as the late 1700s by the American president, Thomas Jefferson, about people living in diverse parts of the same country.

Somewhat like Jefferson's observations on Americans, the population of the entire world can roughly be divided into two parts. The two groups represented are "hot-climate" (relationship-based) cultures and "cold-climate" (task-oriented) cultures. The idea of hot- and cold-climate cultures was first introduced to me by Ricardo Rodriguez, an Argentine lawyer living in Chile. When I went to live in Chile for nine months, I needed his insights to help me make sense of the culture. I had grown up in Israel, lived eleven years in Amsterdam, Holland, and traveled extensively in Europe, the Middle East and Africa. I was from the southern United States originally and had returned there for university and postgraduate studies. Still, I was not fully prepared for the hot Chilean culture. Basic common characteristics had eluded me.

Ricardo would spend hours with me talking about how the people thought, how the Latin leader makes decisions, how the culture worked. In law school he had heard the term "hot- and cold-climate cultures" and he used it to help me understand what I was experiencing. What he said made sense to me: basically that the Latin cultures are "hot," since relationship is the basis of everything, even in the work setting. Northern Europeans are considered "cold," since efficiency is their ruling value.

As I thought more and more about this subject, I began to see that the culture of the "Southerners" in the United States had similarities to other "hot-climate" cultures, such as those of the Latin Americans, more so in fact than with fellow Americans from the northern states. Similarly, the "cold-climate" Israelis of European background had more in common culturally with the Dutch than with their fellow "hot-climate" Jews of Middle Eastern background.

Some countries, of course, did not fit the mould quite as easily. Russia, for instance, has cold weather most of the year. Being primarily agricultural, however, Russians act more like hot-climate folk. When I examined them more closely, I found this true of most rural or tribal societies. Among these are indigenous Alaskans, the mountain village people of the Andes, the Himalayas and other such areas, and Eastern Europeans.

As I have spoken to people from scores of different cultural backgrounds, I have found that identifying cultures in these two categories, hot and cold climates, has provided simple handles with which to grasp basic cultural similarities. It has brought healing, prevented conflict, and helped in planning and problem solving among groups that work cross-culturally. The most rewarding fruit of this endeavor has been to see people come to understand others who are different from themselves, and with this understanding, embrace, rather than avoid, those relationships.

After I gave a lecture on this subject in India, a group of Nepali men came to me. Two had tears in their eyes. The spokesman for the group said, "We want to know why we were never told before how Europeans think. Though they are our colleagues, we have been hurt by them for years. For example, when they asked us to take them on treks into the Himalayas, we would, of course, say yes, as our culture requires. How were we to know that they did not understand our culture? We really meant 'no' but were unable to say so directly because they were guests in our country.

"We did not know they didn't understand our culture, nor that we were really saying 'no.' We would have to leave our families without provision, often for a month at a time, causing great suffering to us and to them. If we had only known these concepts about the differences in the way we think and communicate, we would have been spared pain and broken relationships."

A similar conversation took place in Geneva after I had spoken to a group of professional women. The director of a division of the United Nations in East Africa came to me. Obviously quite emotional, she said, "I'm an African. I have worked among Scandinavians for fourteen years here in Switzerland. If I had only known this when I first came, I would have understood my colleagues' behavior was not rudeness, or rejection, but just cultural difference. To this day, I have very few friendships among them, because I did not understand the basics of their culture."

Who knows why the climate should make such a difference. There are many theories. It may be a matter of agrarian- versus industrial-based economics. It may have to do with the cold weather keeping people indoors more, and thus more to themselves, and less interdependent on their neighbors. Perhaps in the hot cultures there is more "living off the land" and, with it, more interdependence between neighbors, and thus relationships are more important.

I have a theory that the whole world was at one time much more "hot-climate" and that only with the industrial revolution and the artificial imposition of structured time did that change in certain societies. Whatever the case, it happened, and we must face it if we are to get along with our neighbors.

Among the "cold-climate" regions, I would list Canada, the northern states of the U.S., Northern Europe (Switzerland and above), Israel (the Jewish population that came primarily from Europe), the white populations of New Zealand, Australia, and southern Brazil and the white population of South Africa and any other countries or parts of countries largely settled by Europeans, such as Argentina.

Among the "hot-climate" cultures, I would include the Southern United States, Asia, the Pacific Islands, South America (one exception would be much of urban Argentina, which is eighty percent European), Africa, the Mediterranean countries (except the Jewish population of Israel), the Middle East and most of the rest of the world.

Wanda, a farmer's daughter from south Georgia, in the United States, said, "I spent twelve years in the Philippines. From the time I got off the plane, I was at home there. The Filipinos were friendly, unstructured, inclusive and laid-back, like we were back home. Other people talked about culture shock. I wondered what their problem was."

Why was a "hot-climate" Georgian able to find so much in common with "hot-climate" Filipinos? Some clues lay ahead ... .

CHAPTER TWO

RELATIONSHIP VERSUS TASK ORIENTATION

The story has it that President Jimmy Carter frustrated the Western press immensely when he met with Egypt's Anwar Sadat and Israel's Menachem Begin for peace talks. As the media waited with bated breath for their breaking news story, the three heads of state sat behind closed doors drinking coffee. One day passed, then two, with the only news being that of angry reporters wanting to know why no progress reports were coming forth. Meanwhile, inside, the three men were getting to know the names of each other's grandchildren, relationships were being established and trust was being built. After three days, a new relationship was forged, and the Camp David Accords were the fruit.

Jimmy Carter, a peanut farmer from south Georgia is a hot-climate man. He knows all about not rushing the deal. To this day, he carries the honor and respect of being one of the most effective mediators with hot-climate leaders around the world. Whether it is Liberia or North Korea, he has the needed skills. They come naturally to him.

One of the most important differences between the hot- and cold-climate cultures in the work setting is that the hot-climate culture is relationship based, while the cold is task oriented. Coming originally from the South, I understand the concept of relationship-based culture. In the South, interactions between people are friendly and often superficial. Everybody there knows this. When going into a store, it is customary to speak first to be friendly. You might mention the weather, something in the news or something equally impersonal. The simple greeting "Hi, how are you?" will do in many cases.

Once this "feel-good" atmosphere is established, you may then state your business, without being too succinct. It would be acceptable to say something like "Could you help me with something? I'm looking for the hardware section." It would not be acceptable to say something like "I need nails." That would not be considered friendly.

If I were to say to someone in the South, "I just got my hair cut, what do you think of it?" even if my hair gives new definition to the term 'ugly,' the response will invariably be, "It's REAL NAAAS." Translated, this means it's real nice. Truth is not the focus here; keeping a friendliness between us is.

What is the reason for this reaction? All hot-climate communication has one goal: to promote a "feel-good" atmosphere, a friendly environment. The truth can take a backseat to the relationship. No one is willing to jeopardize the friendliness, no matter how superficial, to tell me the truth about my hair. Let me find out how bad it looks some other way.

I told this to a close friend who happened to be a Southerner. She laughed about the hair example and said that though she saw it was true in the South, she preferred to tell it like it is. Only a few weeks later, I came home with a terrible haircut. It was way too short. The same friend insisted she liked it. Then, as I was driving off, she called after me, "And don't worry. Your hair will grow back."

In "cold-climate" Holland, on the other hand, accurate communication is valued. If I asked a friend in Holland what he or she thought of my haircut, the focus on the most accurate answer to my question would be with no thought of how that answer might affect my feelings. The answer might be " It makes your face look fat." If I said, "Well, that hurts my feelings," the person would answer, "What do feelings have to do with it? You asked my opinion. This isn't about you. It's about your hair."

In cold-climate cultures, personal feelings are kept separate from objective issues. A short, seemingly curt answer is often mistaken by the people of hot-climate cultures as being rude or a statement of rejection. They take the curtness personally. In fact, the cold-climate person may be very friendly and warm, but when needing to get a job done or answer a question factually, he or she is completely focused on the task at hand. Rightly or wrongly, personal feelings are not considered to be part of the equation.

If we were talking about personality differences rather than culture, we would call "hot-climate" types 'feeling personalities' and cold-climate types 'thinking personalities.' These are terms used by Isabel Briggs-Myers to describe a difference in personalities in regard to how people base decisions — on their subjective feelings or on their objective logic. [1]

The "feeling"-type person usually has people as the primary focus and combines the task and the relationship so as to be "relational" while getting the job done — even if it means the job gets delayed at times to attend to the relationship. The "thinking"-type person has the task or goal as priority and separates the task from the relationship — even if it means neglecting a person's feelings to get the job done.

Those who have this priority do not mean anything personal by putting the job first. They assume you think the same way. Feeling types also assume that you think like they do, and that's why they are offended by your attitude and actions.

We all have our personality preferences, regardless of our cultures, but our cultures also have personalities. Even if we are high on relationship or "feeling" and we live in Minnesota, a cold-climate state in the United States, we learn to be short and to-the-point in a business transaction. We learn to respect the other person's time and to try to be as quick and efficient as possible out of respect for the person and the task.

Even if we are "thinking" types in our personalities, if we live in a hot climate, a feeling-oriented culture, we learn that it is appropriate to greet with a smile and be friendly. Efficiency is not usually as important as making sure the person feels welcomed and attended to.

When we understand each other, we can make the necessary adjustments.

In the "hot-climate" world, words are often used as a means of establishing a pleasant atmosphere. The literal meaning of the words, therefore, is not nearly as important as the contact established by their use. This is clear in the experience of a friend of mine who was traveling in the Middle East on Yemeni Airlines. A flight attendant came by and said, "Excuse me, sir. Would you like coffee or tea?"

"Oh, I'd love to have a cup of coffee please," he replied.

To this, she answered, "I'm sorry, we only have tea."

For the "cold-climate" person who expects words to be accurate and mean what they say, her answer was mind-boggling. To the Yemeni flight attendant, the words were a mere pleasantry.

1. *Gifts Differing* by Isabel Briggs-Myers, Consulting Psychological Press.

Relationship Versus Task Orientation
Points to Remember

Hot-Climate Cultures:
- Are relationship based.
- Communication must create a "feel-good" atmosphere.
- Though the individuals may be otherwise, the society is feeling oriented.
- Efficiency and time do not take priority over the person.
- It is inappropriate to "talk business" upon first arriving at a business meeting or making a business phone call.

Cold-Climate Cultures:
- Are task oriented.
- Communication must provide accurate information.
- Though individuals may be otherwise, the society is logic oriented.
- Efficiency and time are high priorities, and taking them seriously is a statement of respect for the other person.

CHAPTER THREE

DIRECT VERSUS INDIRECT COMMUNICATION

Another striking difference between the hot- and cold-climate cultures has to do with whether the communication is direct or indirect. In the relational cultures, being indirect is not only a way of avoiding offending the other person and keeping that "feel-good" atmosphere, but also a way of making sure that in no way is one's own preference imposed on another person. The "cold-climate" person, valuing accuracy, will be direct. He will answer the question as efficiently as possible. Here are some examples:

A person is driving to town and a friend asks if he or she can have a ride. The driver, if indirect, will say something like "I'd love to give you a ride, but I'm not sure how much space we will have yet. The car holds five, and six people have already asked. But maybe we can squeeze you in." He is probably sure he doesn't have enough space, but he doesn't dare say so. In contrast, in the cold-climate cultures, saying exactly what you think is a way of respecting the other person's need for accurate information. "I'm sorry, but we're full." That is not rejection. It's information.

Once when I was teaching on the subject of culture in a course in Hawaii, my students were from a dozen different countries. When I talked about the indirect and relationship-based means of communication in most hot-climate cultures, a German man in the class spoke up in disbelief, saying, "I can't imagine this is true. Why would people not just say what they think when asked?"

A Filipino responded, "But it is true. That describes my culture."

The German, in his direct way, said, "Well, I think that is ridiculous."

A little later, I had the class break into groups of four for discussion. There was an Asian couple in the class. Because the wife's comprehension of English was not strong enough to understand the lecture, her husband translated for her. This had prevented her from participating in the class discussion, but I noticed that she was speaking up during the small group discussion.

When everyone had come back together, I thought this might be a great opportunity for the class to hear from the Asian lady, and I asked her if she would report back on behalf of her group. "You can feel free to speak in your language," I assured her, "and your husband could translate for you, if that's okay."

She smiled graciously and nodded, "Be happy to. Be happy to."

An American in the class spoke up and said, "Sarah, didn't you do that wrong? You asked her a direct question, and she is going to say 'yes' even if she means 'no' because she can't tell you no directly. At least, that's what you just taught us."

Cuffing myself on the forehead, I said, "You're absolutely right. I blew it." I turned to the husband and said, "Would you ask your wife if she would mind speaking on behalf of her group."

He asked her in their language, then turned back to me and said, "She asked that she please not be required to share in class. It would be deeply embarrassing for her. She begs not to be required to do so."

The German sat there with his mouth open. He couldn't believe what had just happened.

Here's another case — "Where is the nearest post office located?" Frustrated tourists in Turkey or the Philippines or some other hot-climate culture have asked this question many times and received a very friendly response and even directions. When they followed the directions, however, they discovered, much to their dismay, that the post office was not where they had been sent. Sometimes the village doesn't even have a post office. Sometimes a person is trying to be helpful and cannot bear to disappoint the questioner with bad news, so he or she gives a friendly answer just to create a friendly atmosphere. The answer may not be accurate at all.

So how do you get to the truth? Direct questions should be avoided so that the person being questioned is not shamed for not having the correct answer for you. To find out about the location of the post office, therefore, you may need an indirect strategy.

One method would be to ask a man on the street if he would ask the man on the corner if he knows where the post office is located. In this way, the man on the corner can be free to say to the messenger, "No, man, I haven't a clue where it is." He is free to say this because he is not disappointing a visitor to his country. He is just responding to the messenger. You will discover, sooner or later, that rarely does the direct approach result in the answer you are looking for.

If you have a hot-climate roommate, and you want to know if your music is bothering him, it is worthless to ask directly, "Is my music bothering you?"

The answer will invariably be, "No, it's fine."

If you really want to know, you must be indirect. This could be done in a variety of ways. For instance, you might ask, "What is your favorite kind of music?" If the music is off, you might ask "When do you like listening to music?" Again, the most effective method would be using a third party. Say to the person, "Could you ask Mario what he thinks of my music?" For people of cold-climate background, this seems a dishonest way to find out your information, but believe me, in the hot-climate countries, this is quite acceptable. It is a way of learning the truth without causing offense, and that is of paramount importance.

The people of cold-climate cultures find this round-about way of doing things to be ridiculous. "Why can't they just say what they mean? Why can't their 'yes' be a 'yes' and their 'no' be a 'no'?" they ask. The answer is that the goal of the speaker is friendliness. This isn't about the information; it's about friendliness.

If you were to say 'yes' the first time to the coffee, you would appear too forward, too eager, and the coffee would become the focus, not the hospitality.

As I said before, if you enter a hardware store in Georgia, another hot-climate culture, and say bluntly, "Five pounds of nails, please," you will be considered rude. You are expected to say something pleasant and superficial before stating your business, like "How's it going? You doing all right today?"

If you were to go into a Dutch hardware store talking

that same way, the owner would become irritated because you were taking up his time. There, you can just politely say, " Hello, I'd like five kilos of nails, please." There is no reason to ask how the person is feeling that day. That's none of your business. It's personal information and is reserved for relatives and close friends.

The goal of buying the nails, the task of making the purchase, is the important thing. Short answers in this case are not rude, but are considered part of being efficient and professional.

My life in Holland had given me a well-developed "cold-climate" approach to communication. While in Chile, I would often forget to use an indirect approach. I'd finally arranged with some of my Latino friends that we had two languages: "directo" and "indirecto."

I asked Gladys one day if she'd go into Santiago with me.

"O, si, si quiero ir contigo." (Yes, yes, I'd like to go with you.)

Then I remembered to make sure. "¿Hablas 'directo' o 'indirecto'?" (Are you talking direct or indirect?)

She grinned and admitted, "'Indirecto,' es verdad.

No quiero." (Indirect, it's true. I don't want to go.)

In a rural town in northern Argentina, I had shared these concepts with a group of friends. My hostess, who, up until that point had been warm and friendly, suddenly changed. She started saying no to everything I asked. She opposed me in small ways every time we spoke. After a few days, I was worried. What had I ever done to turn her so against me? Finally, I went to her and asked what I had done to offend her. She answered, "Oh, Sarah, you haven't done anything to offend me. But you said I need to learn to say no, and so I'm practicing." Saying no directly was so foreign to her that she was completely awkward at it.

When I returned to the South a few years later, these lessons came in handy. What finesse it takes to find out what the "hot-climate" person truly prefers! A simple yes or no rarely answers the question.

DIRECT VERSUS INDIRECT COMMUNICATION
POINTS TO REMEMBER

Direct Communication:
- Short, direct questions show respect for the person's time, as well as professionalism.
- A 'yes' is a 'yes,' and a 'no' is a 'no.' There are no hidden meanings.
- An honest, direct answer is information only. It does not reflect on how the person feels about you.
- You can say what you think (nicely), and it will usually not be taken personally.

Indirect Communication:
- It's all about being friendly.
- Every question must be phrased in such a way as to not offend by its directness.
- Use a third party for accurate information if you sense that a direct question will be too harsh, or not get the results you are seeking.
- A 'yes' may not be an answer to your question. It may be the first step in beginning a friendly interchange. Or verbal compliance may be required by the culture. Therefore, avoid yes-or-no questions.
- Avoid embarrassing people.

CHAPTER FOUR

INDIVIDUALISM VERSUS GROUP IDENTITY

Geert Hofstede gives us another serious cultural difference to consider: The individual and the collective in society. (*Cultures and Organizations*, chapter 3, "I, We and They", McGraw Hill, 1991). I refer to the collective as "group" which is found in most hot climate cultures, and "individualists", found more commonly in cold climate cultures.

In most cold-climate societies, from the time children are small, they are taught, "You are an individual. Learn to think for yourself." Children from these countries know that they should have an opinion and be able to defend it. Individuality and independence are affirmed as good qualities. In the United States, one of the founding values of the country is that the individual has rights. "I have my rights" is a phrase you will hear an American say when he doesn't feel he is being treated justly. Another aspect of that individualism can be: "I will look out for myself; you look out for yourself."

In most hot-climate cultures (the Southern United States being one of the exceptions), the opposite is true. Children are taught, "You belong. You belong to a family, to a tribe, to a village. (The Maoris of New Zealand have a saying, 'I belong; therefore I am.') Your actions reflect on the whole group. You must behave in a way that brings honor, not shame, to the family name. We all take care of each other. No one stands alone."

There is a group mentality that says, "We are a community and must share our food, private lives, homes, and even opinions, to serve the whole." This translates into a behavior that is inclusive, not independent.

A common mistake that I have seen made in international gatherings is to ask the people present to give an opinion on a certain subject. The American will readily stand up and give his or her opinion, but the Kenyan will not. He will not speak until he has had time to consult his group. If he already knows how the group feels about a certain subject, he can speak, representing not his own opinion, but the consensus of the group he represents. The result is that one Kenyan voice may represent twenty other individuals, while one American voice may represent just that one person. The leaders of international gatherings may need to find ways to give greater weight to the input of a person representing his group culture.

For example, in a conference where perhaps twenty languages were represented, the principal language was English. All the plenary sessions were conducted in English, as were most of the workshops. The leadership made up mostly of Europeans and Americans, was discussing whether or not to have translation from the podium or just to have simultaneous translations for the various language groups to save time. As various individuals voiced their opinions, it was obvious that simultaneous translation was the preference of the group.

43

Then a man from Bolivia spoke up and quietly explained the difficulty translators had with simultaneous translation. They were only able to hear half sentences because they did not have time to finish translating a sentence before the speaker was on to the next one. He also explained that alternating translation helped those who spoke English as a second language. The time gap after each sentence allowed the person time to assimilate better what was being said. This is true even if he or she does not understand the translation.

The head of the leadership heard the Bolivian, but then said, "Good point, but the majority seem to think it's not worth the loss of time on the podium to have the alternating translation."

What he failed to recognize was that the Bolivian man was representing the majority. The others were not speaking up, simply because they had been represented and did not need, as individuals, to be heard. The people of the "individualistic" cultures all spoke up for themselves, so they seemed to be the majority. The one vote from the hot-climate-culture group must have equaled as many as twenty of the cold-climate votes.

Add this to the dynamic of the hot-climate people

being indirect in their communication and thus more reluctant to state their preferences directly, and we had a poor representation of the desires of the majority of the people.

Individual identity contrasts with group identity in other ways. I was walking in my neighborhood in Amsterdam one afternoon when some young teenage Arab boys started following me and making lewd remarks in Arabic, trying out their ability to be cool with someone who was unsuspecting. To their surprise, I turned around and confronted them, "What is your family name?" I asked.

Shocked that I understood what they were saying, they asked, "Why do you want to know?"

I said, "I want to know which families you boys belong to so I can tell your fathers how you are behaving in public. When they hear how you are shaming the family by your behavior, they will give you the discipline you need."

"No! No!" they pleaded. "Don't tell our parents. We were just joking around and didn't mean any disrespect. We're sorry." And they scampered away.

I had guessed right, knowing they were from an Arab culture, the group identity was probably strong. That meant the actions of the individual reflected on the family, the village, and even the tribe. The individual does not stand alone, and is never the only one affected by his own actions. The mention of their families made the boys realize that they could not get by with bad behavior without it affecting their entire families.

WHEN "INDIVIDUALISTS" VISIT POOR SOCIETIES IN GROUP-ORIENTED CULTURES

In the United States, the economy has been strong since recovery from the Great Depression. Food has not been hard for the average person to find. Food, therefore, has gone from primarily being a source of nourishment to being a source of entertainment. Variety and flavor in foods are important to the Americans. They exercise their freedom of choice when it comes to eating.

When Americans travel to a country where food is still primarily a source of nourishment, they may not realize how offensive it is if they refuse food offered to them just because they don't like it. "Liking" food is only minimally important in those countries. In a poor country or in a poor family almost anywhere, the priority is filling the stomach, not having a variety of or a special taste in foods.

Once while we were preparing a team of American young people to go to a poor country, one young man asked me, "But what do we do if we don't like the food?"

I said, "You eat it. It's about relationship with your hosts. Eating the food is an acceptance of their hospitality, and this has a higher value than the taste of the food."

The individualist is accustomed to deciding what he or she likes or dislikes. In group-oriented cultures, this is not a priority. In many cases, the people do not even ask themselves the question, "Do I like this particular dish?" They just eat it, enjoying it because it is filling them up, or because of the hospitality.

Ricardo, my mentor, once said, "Sarah, in the countries where there has been wealth for several generations, there is an orientation toward comfort and convenience. These countries, however, are relatively few in number. In most countries of the world, the orientation is toward justice and survival. Having what is necessary is important. Having the extra, unnecessary commodities is only for celebrations or some special occasion."

When a host family that is poor puts out a large spread of food for their guests, they may be cooking up several days' worth of food to give the indication of their generosity. They will then feed their family with the food that is left over. Some guests feel that they need to eat it all, but the truth is that leaving some behind might be very much appreciated. It's worth checking out the custom before visiting a home in an unfamiliar culture.

Opulence is more common to places like the United States, where the Great Depression is only a memory for the older generations, and no major war has ravaged the economy in the past one hundred years. For this reason, people from wealthy nations (or wealthy families in any nation) who are guests of the poor should take care to avoid the appearance of wasting food or other precious resources. Unnecessary waste can be painful for some people to witness. They think only of how hard they have worked to have the food they offer.

INDIVIDUALISM VERSUS GROUP ORIENTATION IN A TEAM CONTEXT

For the individualist, being a team member generally means being an equal to the other team members. A leader has a role to fulfill, but probably does not expect to make all the decisions. So, particularly among Westerners, the team members, as individualists, often speak up to their leader or take initiative in the group based on their personal insights into the subject.

Not so, necessarily, with group cultures. With such cultures, the role of the leader is stronger, often more directive. The group members often wait to be called upon rather than assert themselves.

What is sometimes called the "poppy syndrome" may also be a factor to consider. The term refers to the fact that if one member of the group takes the initiative to assert himself or herself, the group will pull him back to see that he fits into the group. In East Africa, I was told, "If a nail sticks its head above the rest, we hammer it down."

People of individualistic backgrounds may not understand this, and will expect personal initiative from someone of a group background. If the person from a group culture has not been given a role to support taking that initiative, he or she may find it extremely foreign. Roles are important, as they provide order for the society.

It is equally confusing when a person from an individualistic culture takes initiative in a team context when it is not within his or her role to do so. If the initiative is seen as inappropriate to the person's position, he or she may be ignored or even rebuked.

A team of young people from individualistic cultures went to Africa for three months of service. The team leader was African. Some of the team members later complained that they were not included in the decisions of the day, nor communicated with personally on what was happening. They were just "told what to do."

As I talked with the leader later, he was surprised to hear that they felt a need for communication. From his perspective, he had told them what they needed to know when they needed to know it.

In group cultures, it is expected that the leader will lead and the team will basically follow. (This, of course, varies with the type of team or group involved, especially within the individual customs of a country.) Team members, out of respect for the office of leadership, are expected to cooperate and not pull against the authority of the leader. This may be a challenge to some who feel they are giving up their identity to do so. To think in terms of "we" instead of "I" can be a major switch for some from individualistic cultures.

The opposite will be true for a person who has left his group culture to visit or study in an individualistic culture. The loneliness of being left to oneself can be overwhelming at first. Also, the challenge of making decisions based on what the individual wants or taking initiative based on the individual's ideas alone may seem rude to them.

A Filipino and an American are sharing a dorm room with three others. The American is playing very loud music. He says to his Filipino roommate, "Does my music bother you?"

It was the wrong question. A person who is not oriented toward declaring his own preference would look around to the others to see if the group in general minds the music. Also, being from a hot climate, the Filipino cannot say directly what he thinks, if it in any way causes an imposition on another. So he naturally responds, "No, no, it's fine."

"Are you sure?" the American asks.

"Yes, of course. It's fine," he is assured. The truth is that the Filipino can't stand the music, but, at the same time, his response has not been a lie. Besides the fact that his culture will not permit him to say so openly, he does not even mind suffering an inconvenience for the sake of the group. It's a normal thing for him to do. The important thing, to him, is the harmony of the group and what the group wants. He was not raised to consider his own comfort first, so he would not think of doing so.

The American, raised as an individualist, was taught to look out for himself and to let his preference be known when asked.

INDIVIDUALISM VERSUS GROUP ORIENTATION
POINTS TO REMEMBER

Individualistic Culture (Cold Climate):
- I am a self-standing person, with my own identity.
- Every individual should have an opinion and can speak for him- or herself.
- Taking initiative within a group is good and expected.
- One must know how to make one's own decisions.
- My behavior reflects on me, not on the group.

Group-Oriented Culture (Hot Climate):
- I belong, therefore I am.
- My identity is tied to the group (family, tribe, etc.).
- The group protects and provides for me.
- Taking initiative within a group can be greatly determined by my role.
- I do not expect to have to stand alone.
- My behavior reflects on the whole group.
- Team members expect direction from the leader.

Note: The Southern United States would be a hot-climate culture that does not necessarily fit the group orientation.

Chapter Five

Inclusion
Versus
Privacy

One of the fruits of group identity common in the hot-climate cultures is inclusion. This is to say that people are automatically included in everything happening in their presence, whether it is a conversation, a meal, a television program, a sport being played or most anything else. This also means that when two people are having a conversation, it is not presumed necessarily to be a private one, and a friend may feel free to walk up and join them.

"Individualistic" cultures value privacy more. This

means that people have a right to privacy, whether in a conversation, a meal or a quiet space to themselves. There is the understanding that an approaching friend would assume the other's need for privacy and would preface the "intrusion" with a phrase such as "Am I interrupting?" or "Do you have a minute?" or "Is this a good time to ask you a question?" This shows respect for the other party.

Most hot-climate cultures are inclusive. In Chile or Egypt or other hot-climate cultures, I can assume I can join in with whatever is going on in my presence, in plans being made and in food being shared.

My sister visited me once while I was staying in Chile. She is a lot of fun, and my friends loved being with her. The only trouble was that I had to translate for her since she didn't speak Spanish. My Spanish had progressed just enough that I could translate for her on a social level.

As we went about town with these friends, my sister made an endless stream of enthusiastic comments on everything she saw. These were directed to me, but because I knew it was rude for the two of us to carry on a private conversation in the presence of my friends, I translated all her comments and questions to the others. They appreciated her remarks and smiled because they were being included in the conversation.

After hours of this, I was exhausted and requested that she be more selective in her comments. It was just too tiring to translate it all. She complied for a while, though it was hard for her to keep quiet about all the new things she was seeing and experiencing. She is a person who likes to express her excitement verbally. I finally turned to my friends and asked, "Would you mind if I don't translate everything my sister says? It's just too exhausting. If it's all right with you, I'll just let you know when she says something important?" They all laughed, saying they understood. We had arrived at a happy compromise.

Among the hot-climate people, there is little distinction between who is a part of an event and who is not, at least on a social level. It is considered rude to mention going to the movies in the presence of someone you don't plan to invite. In fact, in many parts of the world the person assumes inclusion and would be shocked to learn otherwise. In these parts of the world, privacy is not understood. It seems exclusive.

I was invited to the home of an American friend for dinner in Chile. It had been over a year since we had seen each other, and our plan was to catch up on news of mutual friends and share photos. I, for one, was expecting an evening of private conversation.

While we were still eating, a knock came on the door, it opened, and a man came in. He pulled up a chair and joined us. We forgot our previous conversation and talked with this man about local news. Then another knock on the door announced yet another visitor, and this visitor too joined us and the subject of conversation was once again changed. The two visitors stayed until midnight, and we thoroughly enjoyed their company. Our own plans were forgotten.

What seemed strange for me was the fact that my American friend thought nothing of this intrusion. He had lived in Chile so long that he no longer considered our visit a private one. It had become, for him, an inclusive event.

The inclusive cultures see food as something to be shared. The people there would never take out a sandwich in front of others and not offer to share it. I am told that there is a saying in Japanese, "Even if you only have one single pea, you divide it up equally according to the number of people in the room." In these inclusive cultures, there is no concept of "Will there be enough for everyone?" The Maoris of New Zealand also have a proverb: "You bring your basket, I'll bring mine, and together we'll feed everyone." The important thing is that it is shared.

On a bus in Thailand once, with other delegates returning from a conference, I had packed a lunch for the four-hour ride. Having learned about hot-climate inclusion, I brought fruit, cookies and other items that could be shared. About lunchtime, two European men in front of me took out their packed lunches and began to eat. That got me hungry, so I got out my lunch too.

I offered the men some grapes. They said, "Thank you, but we brought our own lunches." They also refused the cookies. Then I got up and offered the grapes to others around me on the bus: Africans, South Americans and Asians. They all happily accepted the offering and then pulled out their own food to share. Soon we were handing around bags of dried figs, potato chips, hunks of bread, cheese and other items. We had a feast that day.

The two Europeans enjoyed their own lunches, but they missed the more important event. It wasn't as much about food as it was about sharing with one another, leaving no one out. It took care of those who didn't have anything by including them in the group. Because everyone shared, we were not aware of the "haves and the have-nots." They were covered by the community. The inclusion value of hot-climate cultures means that no one is left out, no one is lonely.

When I lived in Amsterdam, a common topic of discussion among colleagues was the loneliness of the city. I spent years trying to brainstorm with others on what to do about our feelings of isolation and lack of relationship.

Then I lived in Chile for nine months. At the end of that time I realized I'd never met a lonely person. It was almost impossible to be lonely. People were always dropping in, settling into your kitchen while you cooked, and chatting away. If you wanted to be with people, you just walked out your door and started visiting. If you didn't, you had to hide.

My sister loves people and thrives on "inclusion" culture. She once said, "I could never get tired of people. Just pile them on. Leave me room for oxygen and pile them on." While visiting me in Santiago, she felt ill one evening and went to lie down in our bedroom. A friend came by to see me and sat on my bed to talk. Soon, the room was full, as usual, and some were sitting on my sister's bed as well. No one seemed to notice that she was trying to rest. She loved it.

As a cold-climate person my greatest sacrifice was giving up my privacy, my time to myself. I never knew when I would be interrupted. It seemed exhausting until I got used to it. Then it became second nature to me.

Soon after returning to Amsterdam from Chile, one Sunday afternoon I cooked up some food, which I often do for recreation. I then proceeded to call around to friends to invite them over that evening to eat. Call after call met with disappointment. No one could come. I would get the response of: "I would ordinarily have loved to come, but I was planning to just relax tonight," or "Oh, if I'd only known earlier, but I've taken a bath now and don't want to go back out. How about if we do lunch on Tuesday?" Well, I wasn't lonely at lunchtime on Tuesday; I was lonely on Sunday night. Yet because of the need they had to have planned to come, I was not able to convince a single friend to come over. That's when I realized a reason for loneliness in our well-organized city. What we needed was some hot-climate spontaneous relationship and a little less cold-climate structured privacy.

When I returned to the United States, I missed being with Latinos. In fact, I was lonely in general. I went to the local Huddle House restaurant for a cup of coffee just to be around people. From my booth, suddenly I heard Spanish being spoken. I was now aware of the inclusion principle of hot-climate people and figured most all Spanish-speaking people would be from some hot climate. I greeted the Spanish speakers in their language. I told them I had just returned from Chile and missed hearing Spanish. Just as I expected, the mother scooted over in her booth and patted the seat, indicating that I should join them. I retrieved my cup of coffee from the other table and settled into their booth like an old family member.

They were a Mexican family on vacation in the United States. He was a doctor and had looked forward to this trip for years. He told me, however, that I was the first American to extend a welcome to them. They had been surprised at how private everyone seemed to be. They were not complaining; they were just thrilled to have an American relate to them the way they would relate to a visitor in their country.

In many hot-climate cultures, gatherings outside the workplace are family gatherings. Children are part of the picture — noise and all. This is frustrating for the Americans or Europeans, as they feel the distraction of children running in and out takes away from the quality of the event.

I once attended a meeting in South America where the mothers wanted to be involved in some major decisions being made. Naturally, they brought their children with them, since the concept of getting a babysitter was foreign to most of them. At one point the noise and commotion got so out of hand that the adults were spending most of their time keeping the children in line.

Because it was such an important meeting to these

people, I offered to take the children (all fourteen of them) to my house for a video. When the parents came by to retrieve them later, they thanked me profusely and expressed their amazement at how much they were able to accomplish without the distractions. To my cold-climate values, the task of the meeting was unquestionably the priority. To my Latino friends, being together with the whole family had become the higher value — even in a business meeting. I was in their country, so eventually I learned to tune out the children in order to focus on the discussion.

When traveling in privacy cultures, a common mistake made by those from inclusive cultures is to assume that their children are included in invitations. They have little understanding of "adults-only" events. They need to realize that in cases such as weddings, where children are invited, they are expected to stay with their parents, and if they make noise, they should be removed.

When visiting privacy cultures, people from hot-climate countries should make a point of clarifying whether or not an invitation includes children. It is better to find out ahead of time who is included. To show up with four children at someone's home for dinner, and then discover plates set only for the adults, is an unnecessary embarrassment.

Possessions

In the individualistic cultures, possessions are treated as the personal responsibility of the individual. He is the steward of them, must take care of them, and has the right to share or not share. From a young age the child is taught to take care of his bicycle, his toys, his other possessions.

In the inclusion culture, this is reversed. Most everything is "ours," not "mine." A member of the family will say, "We have a guitar." "We have food in the refrigerator." This "we" will include everyone in the house, not just the residents of the house. "We have tools to use" — regardless of who paid for them.

A student just arriving in Hawaii from China came to his dorm room after his American roommates had already deposited their luggage and left. When they returned, they found their suitcases opened; their clothes were out, and the Chinese student was trying them on. The two North American students went into a rage at this invasion of their privacy, leaving the Chinese young man confused and shamed. His introduction to America was one of trauma and wounding. He was from a culture where (particularly with the influence of Communism) everything was shared. He had no concept of how individualistically Americans viewed their things.

In the worldview of the Chinese student, it was not "I have shampoo," it was "We have shampoo." It was not "You have a suitcase full of clothes, and so do I," but "There are clothes here to be worn. Let's see which ones fit me best."

In many countries with inclusive cultures, I never go anywhere alone. Whether it is driving or walking, someone else comes along to keep me company. If I would insist on driving to the store alone, this would probably be seen as a rejection of the others.

By the same token, if a car is going to town and there

is space available, I know I can ask to go along. I witnessed a man seeking a ride from an American couple on their way to town. They turned him down, wanting time to themselves. Their decision was based on a need for privacy. Nevertheless, the man felt rejected. To the inclusive, it is never "I am going into town," it is "We have a ride to town."

Some excerpts from my personal journal illustrate the conflict:

Yemen, September 14, 1999:

I have had a hard time trying to find time to work on this book. I had to look at my itinerary to see where I might grab some "alone time." I have found it here in Yemen, which is an inclusion culture, but I'm with Westerners who have heavy work loads themselves and who totally appreciate my need for time alone. So my housing is very private, and when I'm not in meetings it's okay for me to stay by myself to get writing done. I go from here to East Africa and will be almost exclusively with Africans, who would probably feel badly for me if I had to be alone.

Uganda, October 1999:

I am in lovely Uganda. I was shown my room. It was simply furnished with a bed and a mosquito net. Next to my bed another mattress had been placed on the floor and a makeshift mosquito net tied to the window to cover it. My hostess said, "Here is your room, but don't worry. I have put a person in here with you so you won't have to be alone."

I smiled and thanked her for her thoughtfulness.

Inclusion Versus Privacy
Points to Remember

Hot-Climate (Inclusion) Cultures:
- Are a group-oriented culture.
- Individuals know they are automatically included in conversation, meals, and the other activities of the group.
- Possessions are to be used freely by all: food, tools, etc.
- It is not desirable to be left to oneself.
- It is rude to hold a private conversation or make plans that exclude others present.

Cold-Climate (Privacy) Cultures:
- People enjoy having time and space to themselves.
- People are expected to ask permission to borrow something or to interrupt a conversation.
- Each person is considered to be the steward of his or her possessions and has the responsibility to maintain and protect them.
- In a community setting, it might be common to label one's food, tools, etc. to set them apart from the group's common possessions.
- It is acceptable to hold private conversations or make exclusive plans with a few people, not including everyone.

Chapter Six

Different Concepts of Hospitality

In the hot-climate cultures, hospitality is the context for relationship. It's a way of saying "I am offering a relationship out of which we can do business." This is not the same as a personal relationship, but it is a relationship nonetheless.

Hospitality always involves food and/or drink, and is usually done in the home. [1] In the United States, it is increasingly common to take someone out to a restaurant to do business or even to entertain a visitor. This would not be considered good hospitality in the hot-climate cultures. It is not personal enough. To bring someone into your home is to say "I offer to relate to you personally."

On a casual day-to-day basis, hospitality may be something as simple as offering a cup of tea or insisting you stay and eat with the family. There is little concept of it being a formal occasion that requires a special menu or cleaning the house first. Spontaneity is part of hospitality. It could mean meeting the need for a meal when it is suddenly needed.

When I first went to Chile, I was looking forward to the hospitality and assumed that I would be invited into the homes of the people. The first month I was there, however, although I was in a small community and people knew I was there, nothing happened. I was crushed by this. I enjoyed interacting with the people during the day, but I wanted very much to be a greater part of their lives.

Finally one day I voiced my disappointment to Ricardo, my mentor. He laughed and said, "Sarah, they are offended that you have not come by. You stay to yourself at night like you don't want relationship. We don't send out invitations around here. You just come by."

"But how can I 'come by' when I don't even know these people?" I asked.

"That's just the way it's done," he said. "Only formal occasions require invitations. The rest is spontaneous."

"But what if people are busy or want to be left alone? How would I know when to come over?" I insisted.

"Sarah," he told me, "you just don't get it. Your coming over will never interrupt them. They will continue cooking, playing with the kids or watering the garden. You will just fit into whatever is going on at the moment. They won't drop everything to sit in a formal living room with you."

Concerning the possibility that people may want to be alone, he told me, "In our culture, people come first, and our own desires come last. We would never forfeit hospitality for time alone."

I learned that he was right. Soon I was dropping in on people, and they loved it.

HOSPITALITY AND TRAVELING

Because hospitality in the hot-climate world is largely spontaneous, there is no thought of "We weren't planning for you, so of course it is appropriate to direct you to a hotel." If a person shows up unexpectedly, that person is fully aware that he or she was not expected, so it isn't a problem. A place on the floor would be fine for most of those who know you are unprepared for their arrival. The important thing for them is to be able to stay with people they know or can trust.

In most hot-climate cultures, hospitality automatically means taking in and caring for the traveler. If you are visiting someone's home, they take full responsibility for your needs. They house, feed and entertain you, and you are not expected to pay for anything. You are under their roof, and this means you should have no needs that they cannot provide. However, it would also be considered normal, even expected, for the traveler to offer a gift to the host.

This leads to serious misunderstandings when a hot-climate person travels to the United States or Northern Europe. Being individualistic, the people in those countries think in terms of the traveler being responsible for his own needs. If housing is offered, that is special hospitality, but they assume the traveler has his own itinerary and plans and even his own means for eating out.

One of the shocks a foreigner encounters the moment he arrives in some cold-climate countries is that he needs money to survive. Even to get a cart to remove his luggage from the airport, he needs money. (Most of the world's airports provide such carts free of charge or have men to carry the bags, and the tipping is left to the discretion of the traveler, but not in the United States.)

Many travelers from hot-climate countries, if they happen to be limited in funds, have saved, sacrificed, and received gifts from family and friends to purchase their airplane tickets. Once they are on the plane, they assume that they are now guests. When their food is provided on the plane, this reinforces their feeling that they will be cared for by their hosts. Little do they realize that many American families have never even considered this as their responsibility.

If a foreign guest is part of an outing to the beach, his friends may suggest going off for ice cream and assume he has cash to pay for his. (This is more common in the United States than in Europe.)This shocks the visitor, for he is unaware that hosts are responsible only for what they have agreed to in advance. The humiliation he feels when standing there with the ice cream, and his friends walking off with theirs, is excruciating. He doesn't have money with him.

In most hot-climate countries, in fact, in most other countries of the world outside of the United States, if someone says to you, "Let's get a hamburger," it means "I'm inviting you to go, and I will pay." I rarely find a visitor to the United States who has not learned this custom the painful, humiliating way. Usually they have finished the meal by the time they learn that they are splitting the bill, and they either don't have the money with them, or they wish they had known ahead of time so that they could have opted out. They were really not interested in eating out and went only because they thought they were responding to an offer of relationship.

Those who are preparing to go to the United States, therefore, must plan to take along some spending money. It will save them much embarrassment and pain.

It they don't have money with them, it can be difficult for them to talk about it with their hosts. It might be advisable for a host to include a small envelope of "entertainment cash" in a welcome basket for a guest whom he knows has little cash with him.

These are simple lessons, but they help us to understand each other in our ever-shrinking world.

1. An exception to this may be China, where the people entertain guests in restaurants more often than inviting visitors into their homes. This might be due to the modesty of their homes or also because Chinese food takes a long time to prepare, and so it's easier for them to entertain in a restaurant.

Different Concepts of Hospitality
Points to Remember

Hot-Climate:
- Hospitality is spontaneous, often without an advance invitation.
- It is the context for relationship (even a business relationship).
- Hospitality usually takes place in the home.
- The host fully takes care of the needs of the guest. The guest pays for nothing.
- A gift is usually expected.
- Food and drink are involved.
- Travelers are taken in and provided for.

Cold-Climate:
- Hospitality is taken very seriously and is planned for.
- It is usually not as spontaneous. The host usually needs advance notice of a visit.
- Travelers are expected to make their own arrangements other than what is specifically communicated to the host ahead of time.
- Guests need to expect to pay for their transportation and restaurants if visiting in the United States. If the host plans to pay, he usually will say so.
- Hospitality is a special occasion, taking the full attention of the host.

CHAPTER SEVEN

HIGH-CONTEXT VERSUS LOW-CONTEXT CULTURES

There is another category of culture that cannot be ignored. It has to do with whether a culture is "formal" or "informal." Edward T. Hall, in his book *Beyond Culture,* referred to formal culture as "high-context" and to informal culture as "low-context." A high-context or formal culture is one that has been around a long time. Switzerland is more than eight hundred years old, and the Swiss have had time to build tradition upon tradition, collecting many rules that everyone seems to know except the foreigner.

Everything matters in Switzerland. It matters how high you grow your hedge. It matters when you put your trash out on the street. It matters that you bring a gift when you visit someone's home. It matters how you dress when you go shopping downtown on a Saturday morning.

In the cities of Switzerland, it is easy to spot a tourist. Middle-aged women, if they are wearing tennis shoes in downtown Lausanne, will not be Swiss women.

In a high-context culture, everything matters. There is a definite protocol for everything — how you eat, how you greet (particularly the way young people address older people), wedding traditions, table manners, who you know ... . You name it, and the high-context community has a rule to cover it. Everything matters.

Another thing that distinguishes high-context cultures is that they have not significantly mixed with other cultures. Villages, consequently, tend to be higher context than cities, as cities tend to collect mixes of cultures. In New York, at home, the Italian family may have its traditions which the children grow up knowing are important, but outside the house — in the school and on the streets — these customs and rules may give way to the mix of other cultures that make up the neighborhood.

If it is customary among Yemenis to require their teenage girls to keep their heads covered, that rule is supported by the community. If a Yemeni family moves to New York, however, their children go to school with Irish, Italian and African-American young people who do not cover their heads. Soon the daughters will be asking if they can wear the head covering only when other Yemenis are around and leave it off when they go out. They want to fit into the mixed culture of the city. Some high-context peoples have stayed together in large cities, creating ethnic neighborhoods, where their high context can be protected to some degree.

Cities that have stayed the same, avoiding a significant influence from outside cultures, are more high context. Damascus, Syria, is just such a city.

Low-context cultures are young, or mixes of cultures. Australia and the U.S. are both less than two hundred and fifty years old and continue to add new ethnic groups. There has not been a monocultural people dwelling there long enough to establish the "high-context" of the white populations of those countries. The indigenous people — the Aborigines of Australia, Native American Indians, and the Maoris of New Zealand are "high-context." They have been there for hundreds of years, as one culture.

The southern Californian culture is an example of low-context, or informal, culture. It is a relatively young society, having been largely populated since the late 1800s. In California, anything goes and nothing matters. It doesn't matter what you wear to church or synagogue. There are few social rules that people are expected to follow. In fact, those who live in California feel a sense of freedom to be creative, start new trends, be different. This lack of context has even made it possible for some who would be rejected at home to make a new start. Interracial marriages, for instance, shunned in most high-context towns, are common and accepted in Los Angeles.

Native Californians often do not understand why such things as "proper" wedding etiquette mean so much to the family from "back East" or the older, more high context states of the United States. With the constant arrival of new people from every possible culture, California continues to be a mix, with no particular culture dictating to the others what is appropriate and what is not. So there is an informality in the language, dress and manners of the Californian that stands out when he is overseas or in a high-context culture such as Switzerland or an African village.

The Jewish nation of Israel is another young culture, just over sixty years old. Its people are completely casual. Government officials in Israel can be found wearing open-necked shirts or even shorts to the office. The military is also more casual than most, with officers and subordinates often addressing each other on a first-name basis.

The reason for all of this is that with the merging of Jewish cultures from around the world, no one culture has prevailed as the one with the definitive etiquette for the country. Of course, there are pockets of high-context culture in Israel, as there are in all countries where ethnic groups choose to live together. These would include the Yemenite, German and Orthodox Jewish communities, among others, each with its strict traditions and rules.

The Arab communities in Israel are more high context however. They see traditions, protocol, addressing elders or superiors by title, as a matter of honor and respect. If one goes to an Arab home for a meal, there are rules to follow. For instance, dressing up is expected, as a way of honoring your host. Bringing a gift, conversing in polite and gracious language and knowing when to leave, are ways as well. In some cases, there are signals you should be aware of. For instance, the serving of the coffee may signal the visit is ending. You would not want to leave until the coffee is served in this case, and it is important to find out ahead of time what the expected protocol is. Can you imagine peace in the Middle East ever happening without the various people first having an understanding of the vast differences in each other's culture?

Korea is five thousand years old. Now *that's* an old culture. Imagine the stacks of traditions and rules that have had time to accumulate there. From the time a Korean child is born, he is constantly being instructed on what is appropriate and what is required in his culture. Authority goes with age and position. Titles —

such as teacher, mister, missus and officer — accompany each person's name, and the given name (first name) is never used without it. Proper protocol is expected at all times.

A Korean going overseas usually considers his customs to be normal. When he encounters the informality of the West, he is often surprised and takes the informality as a lack of respect for himself and others. One Korean friend came to work on an international team in a low-context culture and was shocked to find that everyone was on a first name basis. Even the children called adults by their first names. Staff members called their supervisors (on all levels) by their given names. My Korean friend found this awkward and dishonoring, and attempted to use "Mr." for himself and others, until he finally gave up.

The rest of the staff, although they could not understand this apparent arrogance, complied with his request. Later, however, when he asked that he be greeted when anyone entered a room he was in, this was too much for some of those from other nationalities. Rather than simply sitting down and talking about their own traditions and cultural rules, they argued with him and became angry, and a dividing wall went up.

Another Korean friend of mine came to work cross-culturally in that same country. She knew that it would be difficult, even painful, and the first few years were just that. Soon, however, she learned to change hats. She wore her Western hat where that was appropriate and switched back to her Korean one when around Koreans. The good part about her approach is that she became a culture bridge for other Koreans as they ventured outside of their nation. She did not become a Westerner, but one who knew how to relate to Westerners.

It is important to mention that since the '90's, the culture of Korea has been rapidly changing with international travel, the internet, technology, media, etc. The Korean young person is becoming more westernized. Many say they are a new kind of Korean. Still they know the values of the earlier generations and for the most part are highly respectful towards them.

WHO YOU KNOW

In high-context settings, who you know is more important than what you know. The family tree to which you are connected matters. I learned this the hard way back in my grandparents' hometown in the southern United States. I moved there after knowing the town only through visits to my grandparents. I knew Southerners were friendly folk, so I was expecting to be welcomed with open arms. I was amazed when I went into a place of business and asked to open an account there, only to find that the proprietor was reluctant.

Because I grew up overseas, I no longer had the Southern accent I was born with. This proprietor assumed I was a "Floridian." Because of the growing crime rate in Florida's cities, people there were buying land in our area and moving in. I had heard that outsiders moving into the area were called "Floridians." It didn't matter if you were from New York or China, you were still a "Floridian."

A week or two later I decided to go back in and open that account. When I told the man my intentions, he said, "Well, okay. Give me your address so we'll know where to come for deliveries."

I said, "Do you know where Homer Cook's property is?"

He said, "Well, sure."

I said, "That was my granddaddy, and I live on the back side of his property."

"You're Homer and Annette Cook's granddaughter!" he said. "Why, there's no finer folk in the county than your grandparents. Your granddaddy refinished an antique dresser that belonged to my grandparents and gave it back to us after they died, and it's the only thing of theirs I have. He was a fine man. Sarah, it will be a pleasure doing business with you." I had not changed, but I was now "in context," and suddenly I was accepted.

This is equally true for those moving into high-context settings where they have no connections. In some cases, those who come in the wrong way can remain outsiders for years and even decades.

Some may want very much to be accepted by the locals. They go out and introduce themselves or try to strike up conversations with people they meet in churches or places of business. They may encounter a strong initial friendliness, but often little relationship will be extended to them. The locals don't yet know how these new people will fit into their context. Being introduced by people who carry respect in the community can make all the difference. When you carry their stamp of approval, that gives permission to others to relate to you, even though you are a newcomer.

I have European friends who did it right. They moved to a Middle Eastern city to learn Arabic and needed housing. They knocked on the door of a family in the city, asking if they had a room available. As it turned out, the family did have a room they were willing to rent to them.

My friends later learned that this was one of the oldest families in the city. They had lived there for eight hundred years and had supplied many of the mayors of the city over the generations. My friends came into respectability by association. By being in this family's household, they carried the family name, and doors of relationship were flung open for them.

Within a few short weeks of being in the country, they were more accepted by the Arab society than other foreigners who had been there for years. The secret was being in the proper context.

How You Dress

In high-context cultures, because everything matters, so does how you dress. Even in poor areas of the world, the people dress their very best when going to a meeting, out in public or to someone's home for dinner. For a low-context person, wearing sensible shoes, a rumpled cotton skirt and nice T-shirt to match when traveling may seem adequate. That would be considered an insult by the host in a high-context culture. That manner of dress says, "I don't respect you or your protocol, and I express how casually I take it by not bothering to dress appropriately."

Americans are especially guilty of this. There is something in the mind-set of the American that says being comfortable is of higher importance than looking appropriate. There has been a subtle shift in American attitudes since the sixties. I still remember my grandmother, living in a small high-context town, announcing that she had to go get dressed because she was going to town. Her trip to the post office and bank meant putting on a nice dress, her lipstick, a hat and dressy shoes and carrying a nice purse. If I started out of the house in my play clothes to go with her, and I was dirty or too casual, she would send me back in to put on a decent outfit and comb my hair. Being presentable mattered.

I still remember when flying on an airplane was a dress-up occasion. Men wore coats and ties. Women dressed in their finest. Comfort was not the consideration.

When flying internationally these days, travelers are commonly seen wearing a wide variety of clothing, from dark, formal suits to casual sportswear.. My guess is that the dressed-up ones will be from high-context cultures, and the casually dressed will be from Israel, Australia, the United States or some other low-context country. Today, few American tourists get on an airplane without comfortable stretch clothing and tennis shoes, unless traveling on business. Their casual appearance stands out in stark contrast to the suits and ties and dresses and matching shoes of the internationals on the same plane

Young people in general also dress casually. In most cultures they make up the low-context side of the culture. They may be testing the boundaries of their family's rules, expressing their individuality or mimicking teenage idols of other cultures. Regardless, they often are more open to change, accepting new ideas or new people, simply because they want to know what is outside their context. Usually, once the young people get married and start raising a family of their own, they settle back into their own cultural context, even if they have strayed.

When going into high-context societies, the rule is to look around and see how other people are dressing. It is better to err on the side of formality, so as to show honor, rather than to dishonor your host or the people you hope to relate to. When in doubt, dress up.

Power Distance

Many high-context societies are known to have a greater "power distance" than the more casual low-context cultures. Power distance, a term given by Dr. Geert

Hofstede (*Cultures and Organizations, Software for the Mind*) refers to the lack of familiar relationship between the levels of authority, such as teacher and student, officer and soldier, boss and employee, even parent and child. Usually, the more formal the society, the greater the distance between authority figures and their subordinates. Addressing authority with titles, respect and deference is expected.

This is common in most of the world, but the young societies (such as previously mentioned California or Israel) have a lower power distance. Children might call their teachers by their first (given) names and get by with talking disrespectfully to their elders, and employees might question their bosses openly. This would be unheard of in countries where power distance is great, such as South Africa or the Asian countries. Respect for an elder or someone of superior status is expected in high-context cultures.

The casual friendliness that may be common between university professors and their students in California would be unheard of in China, for instance. Though the younger Koreans are telling me this is true mostly with the older Korean generations only, the youth, too, know how to act when relating to their elders.

The casual American or Australian can offend a Korean by addressing him or her by the first name. Their informality is seen as disrespect.

Regarding communication in the work setting, an Australian team member may feel the freedom to challenge the supervisor or team leader on an idea, simply because, for him, the power distance is not great. He assumes he has the freedom to give his opinion, as one whose opinion is equal in value. A team member from a high-context culture may be shocked by this apparent disrespect.

My American cousin lived in Thailand for a year. In helping a young man with his English lessons, she discovered the teacher had made some grammatical mistakes. My cousin wanted to bring these mistakes to the attention of the teacher, but the Thai student was horrified that she would even consider correcting one of superior status.

When teaching a multi-cultural class in India, I offered an optional workshop one evening. A few people had shown an interest in a subject that was not in the curriculum, so I thought I would open the opportunity to the whole class to go into the subject in detail.

Of the one hundred and fifty or so students, about twenty-five were Koreans. To my surprise, they all showed up. Some were obviously tired, yet they came. Later, I realized they came because the teacher invited them. They could not disappoint the teacher by not coming.

So to avoid the mistake, when I offered an optional course the next night, I said, "It is my request that you not attend my class if you need time with your family or if you need the time to work. If this is not a subject that you have a great need for, may I encourage you to take that time to focus on your other school work. You would dishonor me if you came unnecessarily."

This really threw them off. They laughed, knowing what I was doing. That night, only five of the Koreans showed up for my class.

This was one of the reasons for the indirect communication that was necessary in Hawaii with the Asian woman (see the chapter on direct versus indirect communication). Not only was her communication style indirect, but I was the lecturer and therefore authority figure she felt she needed to obey. I was assuming she would simply tell me if she wanted to speak or not, based on my lower context, low power distance cultural background.

GENDER DIFFERENCES

In the cultures where there is great power distance, the gender difference is also more marked. I learned early on as a Western woman not to try to impose my "freedoms" on women of other cultures. More importantly, I learned to remain unoffended when men of other cultures did not treat me as an equal, as I was accustomed to being treated in my own culture. In low-context cultures, where "anything goes" and "nothing matters," it is not as offensive when a woman breaks out of traditional roles as much as it is in a culture where everything matters, including the strict adherence to gender-defined roles.

When speaking in Bolivia to a crowd of mostly men, I began by bringing greetings from my director, a European man whose reputation they knew well. This immediately put me in context. I was well received, and I think much of it had to do with my being perceived as being under the authority of a male leader. They did not see me as a single woman roaming the world alone. That image would have thrown up unnecessary barriers to my teaching.

I travel alone quite a bit in my work, and when I do so in the areas of the world where women are given a role of submission to men, I work hard at conveying my strong ties to my family, and therefore to male leadership.

In the United States, the higher context towns have been influenced by the cities through the media and through travel, and consequently American towns are now more low-context than they were in the 1950s. My American grandmother's role, however, was clear in relation to her husband and other men. She loved being in the home and finding her identity in her role as a much-depended-upon wife and mother. The power distance between her husband and her meant that his directives were obeyed without much resistance. The role of women in her town has gone more low-context now, and the traditional role of the wife has shifted largely out of the house, decreasing the power distance.

The role of women in high-context societies can be confusing to "liberated" low-context people. The separation of roles in many high-context societies can be perceived by low-context people as a statement of value of the person. The woman seems to have less value because she has the role of being in the home, for instance. But in traveling to countries where there is great power distance between men and women, I find I am more effective in my work if I respect the perception of me as a woman and work with it.

I don't demand to be in charge — even if I am the leader of a team — in a place where women are not usually in charge. I've been known to slip the money to a nineteen-year-old male to pay the bill at a restaurant, just so I won't humiliate him by paying for his meal in front of others. I have also taken a male team member with me in some cases when negotiating with an official, letting him do at least part of the talking, so that the male official does not need to have the awkward situation of dealing with a woman directly.

This sounds like an appalling compromise to my colleagues of the more low-context cultures. I have found, however, that I need to know what my purpose is in being there. It is not to argue about their view of women, but to seek the best way to work agreeably together.

If we as women know who we are, we can honor the traditions of a culture in regard to their gender roles. Their own protocol is important to them, and I must not force my own philosophy on them — regardless of how important it may be to me.

THE IMPORTANCE OF GREETINGS

It would be impossible to say too much about how important greeting people is in high-context cultures. Because everything matters in formal cultures, protocol and greetings are the initial impression, the tool that puts you in context. If you blow that, you blow the impression. It's not a matter of doing a perfect indigenous imitation, but of honoring the other person or group of people by greeting them warmly in an appropriate manner.

A Dutch person doesn't want to be hugged, for example. He wants a firm (never limp) handshake and a good strong voice behind your name.

The Swiss wants the kiss to each side of the cheeks (never on the cheeks). It may sound more intimate, but it actually can be more formal than a strong handshake.

An Arab male greets another male with a boisterous display of affection, with lots of charming words to go with it.

A Korean smiles, stands at a respectful distance and bends at the waist (slightly, if familiar with the person or similar in station or age, and lower, to show more respect due to age or status).

One mistake a low-context person makes is failing to recognize how important it is to at least greet — even if the type of greeting is foreign to him or her. Teenagers often fall into this trap. It is their awkward season socially, so they may tend to mumble their names, not look the other person in the eye or not greet at all. They might just walk into a room and walk right past the host. When taking teenagers on cross-cultural outings, it's helpful to talk about, even practice, the greeting that communicates what they want to say. Remember, everything matters.

Others who may struggle with cultural greetings are low-context people who do not have a background where they were trained in protocol. So going cross-cultural doesn't seem to be such a big deal.

Most high-context cultures are forgiving if the foreigners' greeting is not the same as theirs, as long as the greeting shows respect and sincerity. For fast-moving Americans or Australians, it may mean slowing down and giving the proper time and attention to the proper protocol of greeting.

It should be noted that Geert Hofstede's research has shown that High Power Distant and Low Power Distant cultures do not fall along the same lines, necessarily, as the High and Low Context cultures. His book *"Cultures and Organizations, Software for the Mind"*, with Gert Jan Hofstede and Michael Mindov, (McGraw Hill,

2005) gives an excellent delineation, country by country of how they fall on the continuum, relative to one another.

HIGH-CONTEXT VERSUS LOW-CONTEXT CULTURES
POINTS TO REMEMBER

High-Context Societies (everything matters):
- Who you are related to matters.
- Who you know matters.
- It is better to overdress than to underdress.
- Watch to see how others respond in a situation in order to apply appropriate behavior.
- Remember to honor the people you are dealing with; too casual is insulting.
- Ask a local person who has lived overseas for a while what is important to know.
- Use manners.
- Respect the rules.
- Give attention to appropriate greetings.

Low-Context Societies (nothing matters; anything goes — within reason).
- Who you know matters, but not as much. What you know is more important.
- Do not be offended by the casual atmosphere.
- Lack of protocol does not mean rejecting, nor is dishonoring.
- They do not know what your rules are, so leave your rules at home.
- Address people by their given names unless others use titles.

I'D LIKE TO GO TO AFRICA

Today
I thought
I would like
To go to Africa.

Yes, I will go to Kenya
And see if time
Has stood still
Where at least
The walk
Is on the ground
And all comes
To a sudden halt
At dusk
And sounds
Come from the voice
And travel a mile or two
And strength comes from
The family
Near to you.
Yes, Today
I thought
I'd like to go to Africa.

Sallie Lanier
May 5, 1995

Chapter Eight

Different Concepts of Time and Planning

The cold-climate structure and the hot-climate flexibility also affect the ways we get things done. The cold-climate societies have a goal of being efficient, getting the job done, and planning the job in advance. Hot-climate people tend instead to be responders to what life brings rather than trying to plan life.

I am a Southerner who grew up and worked most of my life in cold-climate cultures — Israel and Holland. My personality is more hot climate, being open-ended, spontaneous and easygoing. However, twelve years of working in Holland taught me to use a time manager. I learned to get to the train on time because it was not going to wait, and to plan my day, my week, even my year.

When I went to live in Chile, it was in response to an invitation to serve as a consultant and trainer to some staff and leaders of a nonprofit organization. I had already decided I wanted to live for a season in the Southern Hemisphere, to learn another language and culture, and this was my opportunity. First, however, I would have to clear my calendar because I was booked a year in advance, and some of my obligations could not be changed.

Although it took me a year, I finally got there, having been in occasional communication with a South American contact person during that year. When I arrived, the leaders who had invited me a year earlier were thrilled, but surprised, to see me. "Sarah," one of them said to me, "how good to see you! What brings you back here? How long will you be with us?"

"A year," I answered.

"A year? That's wonderful. What will you be doing here for a whole year?"

I was flabbergasted by this response. I had resigned my position in Amsterdam, rented out my apartment and closed down my responsibilities for the next year. I had virtually burned all my bridges behind me, only to find out I was not being expected.

When I talked to the leader, he said, "Sarah, I do remember our inviting you, but that was a year ago. We've moved on. I apologize that only one person responded to your correspondence because that person has been traveling a lot, and the two of us have not communicated well." I had a choice to make. I could turn around and go back to Europe, or I could stay on with no defined role.

That was my first cultural lesson. We in Europe can plan our agendas a year in advance, and only a major emergency would cause us to change them. Even then, we would communicate the changed plans. In hot-climate cultures outside the United States, there is more of a spontaneous approach to life and a resistance to nailing down plans a full year in advance, knowing circumstances can change.

In my eagerness to have goals and objectives, the first

morning I went into the main kitchen, knowing it would be a good place to begin learning Spanish. As I peeled potatoes, I asked what the names of different objects were and studiously worked at repeating them over and over, committing them to memory. By the end of the day, I was easily speaking several phrases. I was proud of myself until I learned I had spent the whole day learning Portuguese. The kitchen workers were from Brazil.

In the end, I decided that even if I did nothing more than sit around and drink coffee for a year, I was not leaving. For the next nine months, I often sat around drinking coffee.

It was during those nine months that my friend Ricardo Rodriguez spent hour after hour talking to me about how the Latin mind works and how Latin leaders make decisions. Being a lawyer, he had an analytical mind and was brilliant in his observations of the Western influence in South America, as well as in other parts of the world. In the process, I also learned a good conversational level of Spanish.

Looking back, I suppose that I could have reached

my goals of learning about culture and getting a new language in the planned, structured way of going to a university and paying $10,000, attending class and taking exams. But I still would not have learned the language or culture to the depths I did by drinking coffee.

By being with the people, experiencing life as they did, I "got dipped" and came out with understanding, both in the heart and in the head. I almost threw away this opportunity when things had not turned out as I planned. The plans, if made too important, could have cost me the richest learning experience of my life — the spontaneous, unplanned lifestyle of Chile.

On the other hand, all hot-climate cultures recognize that some areas of life require structure. The military is one example. It's no good to wait until the enemy is coming over the hill to organize a defense.

In the same way, structure and planning help avoid crises and may result in higher efficiency, saving money and effort in the long run. When spontaneous cultures become too easygoing and only react to life, they may miss great opportunities. Therein lies a tension between cultures, each with something to offer the other.

TIME

One of the more common cultural differences people talk about is the concept of time. German punctuality is compared to the Mexican *mañana* (it can be done tomorrow). The hot-climate cultures have the reputation for "always being late" by the cold-climate people, who are viewed as being "neurotically time oriented" by their hot-climate friends.

In a time-oriented culture, events are organized and structured. Their organizer is the clock. Society runs more smoothly with a sense of order, and time has been conscripted to provide that order. Therefore, events are always given beginning times and usually even ending times. This is true of major events like weddings, conferences, worship services and music concerts, but it is equally true of smaller events, such as meeting a friend for coffee or picking someone up to go shopping. Order is provided by a time being set for when the event will happen, and the people involved are committed to being there, ready to go, at that specific time.

This can put people under pressure, and make the

time clock extremely powerful. The pressure is increased when circumstances arise that keep the person from getting to his destination by the agreed-upon time. If the person is late, apologies are always made. The apologies represent respect for the other person and for keeping him or her waiting, as his time has been wasted. Time represents how much a person can "get done" in a day. Remember, cold-climate cultures are task oriented, and time provides a means to get the task done.

The event is a wedding. The location is Jamaica, Zimbabwe, Colombia or the Philippines. The wedding is to be at 2:00 pm. At 1:45 pm, four Norwegians and two Canadians show up to take their seats before the wedding starts. They find the church locked up and no one around, except for some children playing out back.

"Excuse me, kids, is this the place the wedding is taking place?"

"Oh, yes. There is a wedding today."

A bit worried that there really is to be a wedding, the guests wait on the steps.

At 1:55, a group of women arrives with flowers, and

111

they unlock the church and start decorating. A choir master comes in a few minutes later and starts getting out choir robes.

By 2:30, a few people arrive, hanging around and talking outside.

The cold-climate guests have found seats by now and keep looking at their watches, becoming frustrated that the wedding is getting started late, and no one seems to care. What they don't know is that at around two o'clock the bride started getting ready, the preacher started a meal with the groom's parents, and a young man started his five-kilometer walk to the church. Stopped along the way by an old man, this young man takes as long as the old man wants to talk. It would have been dishonoring for him to tell the older man that he needed to hurry.

Gradually, the crowd arrives. The choir is practicing, and those who are choir members join the practice one-by-one as they arrive.

Soon, the choir begins to sing, and the festivities start to come to life.

Around 3:45 pm, the bride and groom finally arrive, and the ceremony begins. By six o'clock, the wedding feast is in full swing.

This hot-climate wedding was an event, and the event began at 2:00 pm. That was when people stopped what they were doing and began wedding activities — getting the church decorated, entertaining the groom's family, and washing the children to get them dressed up for the occasion. The event had begun.

The cold-climate guests were frustrated. They expected the bride to start down the aisle at 2:00 pm. Before two, according to their reasoning, everyone should have been in their places at the church and ready to start the wedding. To the hot-climate people, the wedding did begin at 2:00 pm. The event began with all the activity that surrounded it. The ceremony was only a small part of that event.

Once I attended an international conference where we were housed in the same facility as the sessions. To my surprise, the Africans were the first to arrive in the lecture hall. When a Swiss person said, "I thought African time meant always being late," the Africans an-

113

swered, "No, we are event oriented. We know that the event will start now, and we have come for the event. We don't want to miss any of it."

After living in Chile for almost a year, it finally occurred to me to plan to arrive about forty-five minutes later than I said I would, at a café in town, to meet a friend. I did so, and we arrived almost at the same time. This was after regular afternoons of my getting frustrated that I had to stand on the street waiting for almost an hour every time we met.

You may wonder how I guessed at the correct time to arrive on this particular day. It was a process of thinking as she thought. We always said we would meet at 2:00 pm, and her home was about thirty-five minutes away by bus and metro. That gave her ten minutes to notice that it was already 2:00 pm (time to stop whatever she was doing and go to the next event — meeting me — get on her coat and walk out the door). She was always on time for the event, but the event began at 2:00 when she started moving toward the appointment.

In different countries time is measured out differently. It's always a good idea to observe first and see how it works where you are at the moment. In the cold-climate cultures, people enjoy using their time efficiently. This allows them to get more done and to plan how much they can accomplish, both of work and of leisure.

The orderliness of the German culture is reflected in the trains running on time, the quick, efficient way business is handled, even the quick arrival of your coffee at a restaurant. To show respect to people is to respect their time. To keep a person waiting is to say, "You are not important, so your time is not important. I don't respect you or think you have anything more important to do than wait for me."

In some parts of each society, regardless of the culture, time is highly valued as a sign of competence, integrity and respect. The military in any culture or the corporate executive level of businessmen, for instance, has its own culture when it comes to time and structure. Their survival depends on it.

"Time is money" is a saying in the United States.

Almost everywhere I go in the hot-climate world,

the cold-climate people differentiate between "island time," "African time," "Latin time," "Southern time" and "Western time." There is an assumption that if you are Western, you are time conscious. This is largely true, except for the hot-climate Westerners like the Portuguese, Italians and American Southerners.

Being structured, planned and time conscious go hand in hand. Being spontaneous, unplanned and event oriented do, too. My example in the chapter "Inclusion Versus Privacy" about coming back to Amsterdam after being in South America shows this difference as well. It was the fact that the social lives of the cold-climate cultures were planned. You are invited or you even ask to come by, but always with advance notice.

When living in Europe, I carried a day-timer divided into half-hour blocks from 7 am to 7 pm. There was a page for each day. If a meeting came up, I would check my day-timer. It would tell me whether or not I was free. My pages were pretty much filled up, and I moved from one appointment to the next.

When I lived in South America, I had a page for each month, and those pages were mostly blank. Yet my days were full as I looked back. They were filled with spontaneous events or routine events that didn't need a day-timer as a reminder.

I was spontaneously asked to lecture at the University of Concepción, Chile, and to fly to Bolivia, Colombia and Argentina to teach. I was invited into meetings and asked to help in areas of my skills, and I was also able to do some consulting. However, at the beginning of each month, I could not have told you what I would be doing that particular month. Life just happened, and I responded to it.

Different Concepts of Time and Planning
Points to Remember

Hot-Climate Cultures:
- Are not as oriented toward the clock as cold-climate cultures.
- Are event oriented.
- Are spontaneous and flexible in their approach to life.
- Respond to what life brings.
- Consider that saving time is not as important as experiencing the moment.
- Recognize that structure is required in some areas of life (the military, for example).
- Have informal visiting as part of the event.

Cold-Climate Cultures:
- Are time oriented.
- Are structured in their approach to life.
- Enjoy using time efficiently.
- Try to plan their day, and saving time is a value.
- Expecting the event (dinner, the arrival of a guest, or a meeting) to begin at the time announced. Visiting or informally chatting happens before or after the event.

CHAPTER NINE

PRACTICAL NEXT STEPS

The following suggestions may be helpful in making practical application of the concepts of this book:

1. Look for a "culture interpreter," a person who can explain the culture to you. A fellow foreigner who has already successfully made the transition is often a better coach than a local. A local person does not know which aspects of his or her culture are different from your own, so does not know what to emphasize. A foreigner who has made a few mistakes will remember what is important. Later, a local can possibly give you fuller understanding about the aspects you find different.

2. Before arriving at your host culture, read as much as possible on the history of the people. Familiarize yourself with the varieties of ethnic groups within the area and how they relate to one another. To know that all Arabs are not Muslim or that Lebanese Christian Arabs often speak French in the home might be information you would want to know before arrival. Dutch people in their seventies and older generally view North Americans as heroes because of their role in liberating Holland during World War II. The young people, however, often see North Americans as spoiled and materialistic and can't understand their resistance to conserving natural resources. A study of the history will help give reasons for certain attitudes. Seek out book sources in libraries or the Internet.

3. Once you are in the country of your destination, search out books that other foreigners found helpful for that specific culture.

4. Before leaving home, try to find people from that country who can talk to you about their home. A

positive view is important in adjusting to and accepting a new culture. Native people of that country usually will tell you the parts they love. Based on these previous chapters, ask questions about their culture to see where exceptions to these principles may lie and which principles should be emphasized. Ask them what the major adjustments were for them in coming to your country. That will give you a clue as to what will be a reverse adjustment for you.

5. Try to find out the values of the society. Religion, for instance, is taken very seriously in some cultures and not in others. The movie, "Beyond Paradise," is a story of local Hawaiian teenagers who finally accepted a white boy into their inner circle. He was treated as one of them ... until one day at the beach he wanted to hop around on the ruins of an ancient holy site. When he proceeded against his friends' protests, they not only beat him up but broke off their bond of friendship. He did not understand how important their religious customs were to them.

121

6. Be aware of culture shock and culture stress. The familiar routines of life serve to make things easier. We shop in the same grocery store because we know where things are. We take for granted just how much we depend on routine and familiarity. When we go to a place where everything is different and none of our routines serve us, we attempt to adjust. Often we do it by comparing the new to the old familiar world back home. "This tastes like chicken," "I like that store because it sells British style pudding or Korean style rice." A Kenyan will taste American grits and say, "That is just like ugali." A Mexican in India will look at a japati, hoping for something like a tortilla, and say, "Close enough."

Dealing daily with the unfamiliar means making new decisions constantly. Whether it is a matter of transportation or using a telephone, it all has to be relearned. It all takes energy and leads to fatigue — even discouragement. This is culture stress, which lasts longer than culture shock. Culture shock is that negative impact the unfamiliar world makes on you.

7. Returning home: Once you have adjusted to many of the host-culture routines and practices, it will take the same kind of energy to reenter your home culture. It's called "reverse culture shock." Many are unprepared for the toll it takes on them until things become familiar again. May I recommend the book, *Reentry* by Peter Jordan (Seattle, YWAM Publishing: 1992) as an excellent resource. Read it before returning home, to know how to prepare for your reentry, and particularly the reentry of your children.

8. Look for others who have traveled, or even better, for people from your host culture once you return home. Debrief with them. It is rare that a person from your home culture will want to hear all your stories or even understand your need to share them. You are the one who left, and life continued on at home. Over the years, I learned, as I visited my beloved grandparents in the States, that the way to be a part of their lives was to listen to their local news, entering their world. They were not able to identify with my foreign world, and I learned to accept that.

9. Learn phrases in the local language. Even a small attempt is better than none. It means you value the people you have come to work among. I asked some Pacific Islanders working in Canada what they wish they'd known before coming. They all said, "We wish we had learned English. It would have meant all the difference in the way we bonded if we could have built relationships with the people immediately. Once we were here, it took all our energy just to adjust. We were too tired at the end of the day to learn the language."

10. Finally, go listening, observing. Don't pass judgement until you have discovered the reason behind the people's "strange" habits. Assume the highest about them. Assume they know what they are doing and their behavior is founded in experience and their belief systems.

Once on a trip through the Sinai desert, a young man asked our guide why the Beduin Arabs wore so many clothes. Given how hot it was in the desert, this seemed foolish to him. The guide said, "The robes allow air flow which cools them. The sleeves cover their entire arms, keeping them from dehydrating from too much moisture coming off the skin. The headdress is loose, allowing air to circulate around the neck, cooling them. Their clothing is white, reflecting the sun. Wisely, they sleep during the hottest part of the day. And besides, they've been here a few thousand years, so don't you think they would have come up with the best ways to survive this desert?" The desire will be to change your host culture when you see them "doing it wrong." Remember what you have come for, and stick to those goals until you have earned the right to be heard.

Once I was in charge of cooking for a group of twenty people on a work project. A lady who spoke no English was helping me in the kitchen. I had bought a supply of potato peelers once I noticed that people used knives instead. I saw how much of the potato was being wasted with the knives, so I thought I would improve things. As my translator tried to help the lady understand my instructions on how to use the peeler, she finally said, "Sarah, can't you just let her peel the potatoes like she has for generations?" I put the peelers away.

Chapter Ten

In Conclusion

With a little understanding, much conflict can be avoided between people of diverse cultural backgrounds. My hope is that in considering the fact that there are some simple categories to use for broad strokes, you can then fine-tune your knowledge of a new culture.

Not all of these attributes I have mentioned are consistently present in all hot- and cold-climate cultures. One person even suggested that I use the term "hot/tribal" people versus "cold/urban" people, the reason being that many tribes in the cold mountain regions of the world behave as hot-climate people, while many city dwellers in the hot countries of Brazil and Argentina may act more like those from cold-climate areas.

Also, many individuals act very differently from their own cultures because their personalities may fit the opposite types of cultures. The important thing is to ask oneself, "What are my own cultural habits? And are they suitable for the culture I am going into?"

We are all a bit ethnocentric, thinking our way is a bit superior to someone else's. If we can get beyond that, we'll find we can begin to learn, respect and enjoy the differences. Soon, what seems foreign will become familiar. And we'll find we have much in common.